AT SCHOOL

INVADER

This is Miss Harris's classroom.
The children aren't here yet.
Rrrrring! The school bell goes off.
The children will arrive in a minute.

aquarium

sponge

ruler

exercise
book

school bag

Plink and Plonk are happy.
They are the two goldfish.
They know that they will soon be fed.

drawings

globe

waste paper
basket

desk

pencil case

ball

At the beginning of each day
the children play some music.
They have a proper little band.
John plays the triangle and Lee bangs
two cymbals together with all his might.

John

triangle

drum

cymbals

xylophone

Lee

Valerie plays the recorder and Sarah sings a pretty song.
What about you? Which musical instrument do you like to play?

the scales

Sarah

recorder

stool

Valerie

"Look at this. What is this flower called?" asks Valerie.
"It's a violet," shouts Lee, splashing through a puddle.

tree

nest

robin

leaf

violet

Sarah likes collecting fir cones.
Did you know that fir cones can tell you
what the weather will be like?
They open when it is sunny and close up
when it rains.

fence

fir tree

fir cone

puddle

tortoise

After playing in the school garden,
the children have a nature lesson.
Valerie draws a beautiful flower
for Miss Harris.
Does it look like the violet she found?

greenhouse

seeds

earth

leaves

Sarah has planted a flower in a pot.
She puts it in the little greenhouse so that
the plant will grow more quickly.
Lee finishes his nature scrap book.
Look at the leaf he has found.

poster

watering-can

flowerpots

scrap book

At playtime the children like to take
some toys outside.
John is playing skittles.
He is sure to knock them all down
with his third ball.

ball

spinning top

skittles

marbles

playground

Lee is playing football.
He kicks the ball as far as he can.
Look out, John! It's going to hit you!
Sarah loves to play hopscotch.
1, 2, 3 - hurrah! She's done it!

skipping rope

hopscotch

The children do exercises in the gym.
They can choose what they want to do.
Valerie is trying to jump over the horse.
Sarah does a head-over-heels.

gym

shoe bags

racquet

vaulting horse

Lee is balancing on the beam.
He is trying to walk all the way along
without falling off.
Have you ever tried to do that?

bars

beam

mat

Now the children have a quiet time.
The teacher is reading a story about two
children who travel to far-away lands.
"Can we look at the pictures?"
Lee and Valerie ask Miss Harris.

bookcase

stool

Sarah does not want to read.
She wants to finish her jigsaw puzzle.
Can you help her to put the last two
pieces in the right places?

calendar

lamp

plant

books

book

mat

jigsaw
puzzle

Mmmmm! It's lunch time!
John has a cheese sandwich but
he doesn't like it at all.
"You have to eat it," says the teacher.

dining room

clock

sandwich

teacher

apple

spoon

Lee has drunk a huge mug of milk.
He puts his mug on the table.
He will wash it up after lunch.
Oh dear! Valerie has spilt something.
The teacher will help to clean it off.

cups

mug

teapot

bottles

stain

stool

Today it is Sarah's birthday.
She is wearing a yellow crown.
Look at the candles on the cake.
How old is Sarah?

candles

cake

balloon

trumpet

lemonade

glasses

The other children are going to give
Sarah a present.
They have got her some building bricks.
Sssh! Don't tell! It's a surprise!

crown

lantern

present

Lee has put on an old shirt.
He is doing some finger painting.
Look at the hand prints he has made.

crayons

finger painting

paper

stool

Sarah likes to do cutting out, and Valerie
is drawing a picture.
What is John doing? He is going to build
a big house with modelling clay.

paint brushes

modelling clay

 glue

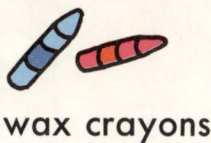

wax crayons

This afternoon, the children play
in the big sand pit.
"Look, Miss," says Sarah. "I have made
some pretty paper flowers."
"That's very good," says Miss Harris.

teacher

flag

sand

spade

Valerie builds a sand castle.
She piles the sand higher and higher.
"Wait for me. I'll help," says John.
"But first I've got to put the ball
in the trolley."

ball

paper flowers

rake

trolley

The children are dressed up.
They are practising for the school play.
John is a cavalier.
Look out! He is holding a large sword.

feather

hat

sword

cavalier

wand

tights

belt

shoes

bow

fairy

Sarah is dressed up as a fairy.
She would really love to be able
to make spells with her magic wand.
All the time, Lee the Red Indian is
galloping around on Fury, his horse.
What do you think Valerie can be?

puppet theatre

dressing-up
clothes

crown

horse

arrows

Red Indian

The children play before school ends
for the day.
Valerie climbs on the rocking horse and
goes for a long ride.
Lee finds the building set and makes
a strange machine.

balls

mask

train

rocking horse

Boo! Sarah made everyone jump!
Look at that horrible mask.
Now the children must go home and
have some tea.
They will be back at school tomorrow.

doll

building set

doll's house